First paperback edition November 2019
Visit the authors website at
www.sheppersonandshepperson.co.uk

While the author has made every effort to provide accurate internet addresses
at the time of publication, neither the publisher or the author assumes any
responsibility for error or for changes that occur after publication. Further, the
publisher does not have any control over and does not assume any responsibility
for author or third-party websites or their content or services.

Printed by Printpoint Carlisle Ltd UK
ISBN: 978-1-907931-92-5 (paperback)

My Beloved speaks and says to me, rise up my love, my fair one and come away. For behold the winter is past; the rain is over and gone. The flowers appear on the earth; the time for singing has come, and the voice of the turtle dove is heard in the land.

Song of Solomon 2:10-12

To those wondering around in the wilderness of life, the Bible says of Jesus:

> *The spirit of the Lord God is on me; because the Lord has anointed me to preach good tidings to the meek; He has sent me to bind up the broken hearted, to proclaim liberty to the captives, and the opening of the prison to them that are bound.*

> *To proclaim the acceptable year of the Lord, and the day of vengeance of our God; to comfort all that mourn;*
> *To appoint to them that mourn in Zion, to give to them beauty for ashes, the oil of joy for mourning, the garment of praise for the spirit of heaviness; that they might be called trees of righteousness, the planting of the Lord, that He might be glorified.*
> *Isaiah 61:1-4*

> *To those that are thirsty God said, "Listen, everyone who is thirsty! Come to the waters; and he who has no money, come, buy and eat. Yes come buy priceless wine and milk without money and without price" [simply for the self-surrender that accepts the blessing]*
> *Why do you spend your money for that which is not bread, and your earning for what does not satisfy? Listen closely to me and eat what is good, and let your soul delight itself in fatness" [spiritual joy]*
> *Isaiah 55:1-2*

I will open rivers on the bare heights, and fountains in the middle of the valleys; I will make the wilderness a pool of water, and the dry land springs of water.
Isaiah 41:18

This is a timeless word of healing and restoration, but also a very 'now' word from the heart of God. It resonated with me and my own path till now of healing and restoration, but also, I will be using it as a tool to give to others to help them walk through their own personal path to freedom and wholeness.

Sandie Wilson, Creative Artist

CONTENTS

Dedication

This book is dedicated to my family. To David and Anthony. To Mum and Dad for their unwavering love, commitment and prayers. To my sisters and brothers, Winnie, Carol, Linda, Paul and Junior. You are my special gifts from God and role models.

I am so privileged and blessed to have you in my life and to be loved by you. I salute you.

Acknowledgement

To my Lord and Saviour Jesus Christ. To Him be all the glory. Thank you for the privilege serving you.

To those I have known throughout my life who have given themselves to nurture, grow, support and encourage the gifts within me in anyway, thank you. To the Pastors whose call on their lives continue to inspire me.

To my praying friends.

Foreword

Hidden Moments is a book in season. So many people in society today carry wounds in their hearts and souls that have become buried in the fabric of their lives, built on and carried as attempts are made to move forward. They are often, but not always, forgotten about waiting to surface and affect decision making, relationships and peace of mind.

Hidden Moments reveals God's heart of love towards us in our hurting places and offers tried and tested solutions and pathways to healing that are found in the Bible. Each chapter ends with a practical prayer to help you along the journey to wholeness.

This book is written from God's heart to your heart.

Pastor Sandy Jamieson, Lighthouse Church, Dumfries, Scotland

Introduction

*Look I am sending my messenger before you and he will prepare
your way. He is a voice shouting in the wilderness 'Prepare a
pathway for the Lord is coming! Make a straight road for Him'.
Mark 1:1-3*

We hear so much nowadays about being fit and healthy in all areas of our
life and everyone seems to want to tell us about our mind, body and spirit
and the importance of the correct balance between them. This is great
news for those who are searching and striving to be the best version of
themselves and to be in the place where they can both give and receive
from a place of wellbeing and completeness. But what about those who
are not there yet, or have been there in the past and are journeying back
to the place called there? In making a decision to embark on the journey
we often have an indication of what is wrong and an idea where we have
been wounded or hurt. However, knowing is one thing, locating its root
is another and how then to mend it is quite something else.

I've learnt in life that even though God wants us to be whole, and what I
mean by that is complete and not lacking in any way, He also wants us to
take part in the process.

In the Bible, blind Bartimaeus had to raise his voice, Miriam had to stay
focussed as she waited for Moses to return form the desert to free the
Israelites, the woman with the issue of blood who was losing life had to
press against the crowd and go where tradition said that she was not
allowed, Nicodemus, although he didn't want to be seen still had to
sacrifice sleep and go at night to find Jesus to get the deepest questions of
his heart answered.

This book is about how God breaks into the ordinariness of life to heal
the parts of us that are broken and how He lovingly puts us back together

again. It's about how He redeems, recovers, resets and mends us so that we can express the real us that we often cannot see.

Like the Roman Centurion, a man with earthly authority in one of the most successful empires of all time, went to Jesus on behalf of his servant who was sick, I pray that Jesus will heal everyone who reads these pages and that they will be set free to reach the fulness of their potential in Christ Jesus. I pray that He will make your crooked paths straight and take you by the hand and lead you to your best future.

CHAPTER 1
He heals the broken hearted

He heals the broken hearted and binds up their wounds
[curing their pains and their sorrows]
Psalm 147:3 Amplified Bible

A Broken Heart

Many years ago, when dreams were the bread and butter of my life, when I didn't know the difference between hope, certainty and expectation and would wake up every morning on tiptoes, almost too excited to sleep, my life shattered when my marriage crumbled. Walking through the maze with its twists and turns of numbness and pain, life stopped.

> The eternal God is your refuge and dwelling place, and underneath us are His everlasting arms. (Deuteronomy 33:27)

In many ways that is when life began in earnest and I started to experience what I have now come to know as God's grace on another level. The Bible tells us that 'The eternal God is your refuge and dwelling place, and underneath us are His everlasting arms' (Deuteronomy 33:27), He protects us. In Psalm 91:1, God tells us that we can rest under His Almighty shadow, under the shade from the heat of life, and that He will cover us. I'd always heard about how God 'carries us', well I was carried. I can't remember walking through each day, but I do remember going through the motions and family underpinning me and keeping me hemmed during my many times of teetering and falling. The whispers of love that soothed my aching soul. The true friends that stood by me and how God used them to apply that balm in Gilead, that the Bible talks about.

1

Early one morning during prayer, I got up off my knees and sat in the silence. It was whilst drawing breath before facing another day that the Lord showed me a picture I will never forget. I was stood crying alone, and in the distance, there was a lone figure following in my footsteps stooping down and carefully picking up the broken pieces of me. I wept. I always knew that I was not alone, but what I didn't know was that through my brokenness every fragment of me was being collected. I would be made whole again, I would not be lost.

The Lord has put me back together. There is a song that says "He took the pieces and put them all together, He took the broken pieces of my life, took what was wrong and made it right." Looking at me today, you would not have known my story. But I share this with you so that you too can be healed and restored by Jesus.

It is true, God does heal the broken hearted and He binds up their wounds, curing their pains and their sorrows.

Call to Action Prayer

> Father God, I come to you in the name of Jesus. I believe that you exist, so I ask you to heal my broken heart and restore me back the whole person that you intended me to be. I give you my hurts and pains, disappointments and all my brokenness that I don't know how to fix and ask you to step in and help me. Thank you for hearing me. Amen.

Notes

A Broken Mind – The thoughts and intents of the heart and mind

Have you ever heard the phrase 'get a grip' meaning get a hold of the situation, get to a place where you understand what is going on so that you can do something about it? Well, what if you haven't got the mind to get hold of it? A broken heart also means a broken mind, those who have been crushed mentally by the pressures of life. There are many ways to be crushed: mentally, physically, emotionally and psychologically to name but a few.

> The man of God helped the woman to see things from God's perspective and gave her an exit strategy, a way to get out of her situation.

The bible tells us of a man who lived in a graveyard and couldn't think for himself, in fact it says that he was not in his right mind and unable to think straight. It's interesting to note that the Bible doesn't tell us what had caused him to be in this state. It would seem that the cause is of little significance otherwise we would have been told. In much the same way, how the broken mind was caused is of no consequence to Jesus in relation to His ability to fix it. Whatever the cause, Jesus healed him and he was 'clothed and in his right mind' and able to make decisions for himself again. It would seem to me that God is saying that no matter what your history is or what your present looks like now, He has the power, ability and is willing to heal all brokenness of mind, distorted perceptions and behaviours that limit us in life. Amazing.

There was a woman who had lost her husband, was in huge debt and was about to lose her sons to the money lenders. In absolute desperation she asked someone who knew God for help. He asked her to think about what she had in her house or, in other words, what she had in her possession. She took an inventory of what she had, and I would imagine it wouldn't have taken too long because she couldn't raise funds to save her children from slavery. As the story unfolds, we find that she had overlooked the value of something that she had owned all along, a pot of oil. The problem was that she couldn't recognised its value or know what to do with it. The man of God helped her to see things from God's perspective and gave her an exit strategy, a way to get out of her situation. It was a financial strategy that would involve the whole family in its outworking. The woman was told to go sell the oil and pay her debt, and she and her sons would be able to live on the rest (2 Kings 4:7). As she followed his instructions, she not only paid off her debt but had enough to live on the rest. Notice that when the answer came, the debt had to be paid off first. This ensured that she and her sons could not only live on the rest but could live in freedom without fear of the future. God wants you to live in freedom.

Call to Action Prayer

The spirit of the Lord is upon me because He has anointed me to preach the gospel to the poor; He has sent me to heal the broken hearted, to preach deliverance to the captives and recovery of sight to the blind, to set at liberty them that are bruised. To preach the acceptable year of the Lord.
Luke 4:18

Father God, I ask you to heal me where I have been crushed by the mental pressures of life and help me to see things from your perspective. Help me to see where I have overlooked the solutions and answers that you have placed in my life. I forgive those that I have refused to forgive and those that I blame for where I am today. Please forgive me and help me to work with you to mend my broken heart, in Jesus name. Amen.

Notes

Notes

Notes

CHAPTER 2
The secret place in a public setting

"Fear not you have nothing to fear, for I am with you; do not look around you and in terror and be dismayed, for I am your God. I will strengthen you and harden you to difficulties, yes I will help you. Yes, I will hold you up and retain you with My right hand of rightness and justice."
Isaiah 41:10 Amplified Bible

The Bible tells us that the fear of man is a snare. It also tells us in 2 Timothy 1:7 that God has not given us a spirit of fear and timidity but of power, love and self-discipline, some versions say a sound mind. It's so easy to say these verses over to yourself time and time again, and I did. One of my favourites verses is He whom the Son sets free is free

> The fear of man brings a snare but whoever leans on, trusts in, and puts his confidence in the Lord is safe and set on high.
>
> (Proverbs 29:25)

indeed, and I believed it then as I do now. But fear seemed to be able to walk in and take top spot whenever it felt like it. It wasn't that I hadn't accepted what God said as truth but there was something on the inside that seemed to be able to choke the word whenever it chose to and 'keep me in a place of restriction' instead of the freedom I craved.

Walking up the stairs on the way to work one day, I found myself asking God to heal me in the places I knew nothing about. I couldn't name or locate them because I didn't know where they were hiding, but what I did know was that they were there. I was being healed from the inside out, I could feel it. Over the next 12 months my fears and who God said I was had a show down. God placed me in positions that forced me out of my comfort zone, present at events that I would normally sit back in and an opportunity to give my first guest speech about breaking through barriers to educational and life success.

During this time, I was invited to attend an interview which involved an overnight stay at a hotel. For the first time, I sat in a busy restaurant, at a table by myself and enjoyed a meal without feeling out of place. That night back in the hotel room as I was making final preparations for the next day, I listened to Tasha Cobbs singing "there is power in the name of Jesus to break every chain, break every chain, break every chain". As I listened and tonged my hair, the presence of God filled the room and broke strongholds in my mind and spirit. I was overwhelmed by His company and knew that historical chains had been broken off my subconscious mind and that I would never be the same again. No room here for fear. I didn't get the job, but I got something far more valuable and permanent, my freedom to be who and what God wanted me to become.

A year earlier, I had listened to a song called *Hello Fear* by Kirk Franklin but couldn't connect with it. It talks about fear being a person that comes knocking at the door and taking a place at the table, then one day his place is taken by Grace, God's grace. When fear tries to come back it is told farewell, goodbye, so long and that the person is enjoying not being a prisoner and instead remembering their true identity.

Call to Action Prayer

*God has not given us a spirit of fear and timidity but of power,
love and a sound mind*
2 Timothy 1:7

Father God I come to you on the basis of your Word and I bring to you every fear that I have in my life. Fear of people, situations, sickness, relationships and failure. I accept that you have not given me the spirit of fear but of power, love and a sound mind. I am sorry for believing fear more than believing the truth of your Word. I exchange my spirit of fear for your spirit right now and ask you to help me to live in the freedom that you have planned for me, in the name of Jesus. Amen.

Notes

Notes

Notes

CHAPTER 3
The heat is on

But He knows the way I take; when He has tried me I shall come forth as gold.
Job 23:10

My heart leapt with excitement when I heard that this was my time of incubation. All I could think about was the warmth and protection of that incubation chamber and being cushioned and protected from all the ills of the world. It was my appointed time for change and I was going to make the most of it.

Little did I know that incubation was code for 'the heat is on'. I was the cake in the oven, the door was shut and, although the door was not locked, there were no handles on the inside! In the months that followed I was betrayed, favoured, promoted, rejected, isolated and humbled. I remember the night before it all began knowing that a test was coming and that there was no escape if I wanted what was to come out on the other side as a better me, it was necessary. I would have to trust God to guide me through it. I cried, and then turned and faced the wind.

These trials are only to test your faith, to show that it is strong and pure. It is being tested as fire tests and purifies gold and your faith is more precious to God than mere gold. So if your faith remains strong after being tried by fiery trials, it will bring you much praise and glory and honour on the day when Jesus Christ is revealed to the whole world.

(1 Peter 1:7 Life Application Bible)

In the months that followed, I felt like I was an observer of someone else. I was sat in the front row of a cinema and too engrossed to eat the

15

popcorn! On reflection, I can see that I was being prepared and 'told the end before the beginning'. Isaiah 41:10-11 was my constant meditation.

> *Fear not, there is no need to fear, for I am with you; do not*
> *look around you in terror and be dismayed, for I am your*
> *God. I will strengthen you and harden you to difficulties, yes*
> *I will help you; yes I will hold you up and retain you with*
> *my victorious right hand of rightness and justice.*

> *Behold, all those who are enraged and inflamed against you*
> *shall be put to shame and confounded; they who strive against*
> *you shall be as nothing and shall perish.*

God didn't tell me that I wouldn't have to go through it but was gracious to remind me that He was with me and the incubation was necessary so that I could be strong and 'hardened off' to difficulty.

Incubation is about becoming who God made you to be. In Psalm 66:10 it says "For you have tried us O God; you have refined us as silver is refined". I've heard it said that a prebaked cake is just a collection of ingredients that have been placed in a bowl and blended together by beating. Great potential but still raw and inedible. In the heat of an oven a transformation takes place and when left at the right temperature for the correct amount of time, something smelling seriously good and tasty emerges. Unrecognisable in look and consistency to its raw self.

The Lord never left my side, and He did hold my hand but most of all He carried me. The Bible tells us that God is no respecter of persons, so I know that He will do the same for you if you allow Him to.

Call to Action Prayer

But He knows the way I take; when He has tried me I shall come forth as gold.
Job 23:10

Father God I know that you know everything and the way that I take. Please help me to trust you as I go through this difficult time in my life. Help me to always remember that you are constantly looking out for my best interests and to remember to walk in love. I look forward to becoming the full expression of the person you created me to be, in Jesus Name. Amen.

Notes

Notes

Notes

CHAPTER 4
I'm tired of crying… for what I'm not praying about

Go up to get ointment, O virgin daughter of Egypt! But your many medicines will bring you no healing.
Jeremiah 46:11

Jeremiah Chapter 8 verse 22 says, "Is there a balm in Gilead? Is there no physician there? Why then is not the health of the daughter of my people been restored?"

> My tears have been my food day and night…
>
> (Psalm 42:3)

There are wounds that are so deep that although you think that you have gotten over the issue, remain deep within your soul. The part of you that affects and if toxic, infects every part of your life. It colours how you see and do life.

One morning when I was praying, I said to the Lord, I'm tired of crying for what I'm not praying about. The Lord's reply was, is there a balm in Gilead? The Lord had been healing me from disappointment, and on the surface of things, my life was certainly moving forward. I cried some more, dried my eyes and got on with the day.

An evangelist was preaching that night at a local church and I felt an urge to attend. I went with a dear friend and towards the end of the meeting an invitation was made for those who wanted to be healed from sickness in their bodies. I went forward, even though my request did not fit in with the call. I will never forget the evangelist's words, he said "You will never cry for that thing ever again". All I can say to you is that something broke in my spirit and mended deep within the core of who I was. I have never cried for that 'thing' again.

21

At the end of the meeting the minister explained to the congregation that the following evening he was going to pray specifically for emotional healing.

My question in the morning had been answered by nightfall and I am living proof today that there is a balm in Gilead and His name is Jesus. Ask Jesus, He'll heal you too.

Call to Action Prayer

> *He was wounded for our transgressions, bruised for our iniquities and the chastisement that brought us peace was laid upon Him and by His wounds we are healed.*
> *Isaiah 53:5*

Lord Jesus I thank you that you were wounded and crushed for my rebellion and refusing to do things your way. Thank you for taking my punishment so that I could live in your peace. Thank you for taking my wounds so I can be healed in every way. Forgive me for not recognising what it cost you to set me free. I ask you to heal me in my broken places. You created me and know me, so I receive your healing in exchange for my brokenness. Amen.

Notes

Notes

CHAPTER 5
Let not your heart be troubled

Do not let your hearts be troubled (depressed or agitated). You believe in and trust and trust in and rely on God; believe in and trust also on Me. In my Father's house there are many dwelling places (homes). If it were not so, I would have told you; for I am going away to prepare a place for you.

John 14:1-2 Amplified Bible

I couldn't tell you the amount of times that I've read those verses or heard them quoted over the years and although I understood the words… I couldn't say that I have always lived them.

> God does what He says.

Many years ago, I gave up a full-time job and moved into teaching part time at a local college. That doesn't sound like anything you might think, however, I had a mortgage, an expensive car to pay for, was not qualified to teach, there was not guarantee of extra hours and I was single. After handing my notice in, I remember waking up in a cold sweat thinking, what on earth am I doing leaving a 'yours until retirement' job with all its securities?

That morning, I read *"Do not let your hearts be troubled (depressed or agitated). You believe in and trust and trust in and rely on God; believe in and trust also on Me."* *John:14.1.* I heard them again at the Sunday morning service.

Over the months I saw God provide for my every need, and although there was more month than money and bills than finance, all the bills were paid and not one car payment was missed. In fact my boss commented that she didn't know how I could live like I lived on what she paid me! The truth of the matter was it didn't make sense to me either, all I knew was that I was living on God's provision and not hers.

I'm reminded of when Jesus rejoiced in Luke 10:21 after the 72 believers came back from their mission trip that He had sent them on. On their return they were rejoicing that the spirits were subservient to the name of Jesus. He said to His Father "I thank you Father, Lord of Heaven and earth, that You have concealed these things from the wise and understanding and learned, and revealed them to babes (the childish, unskilled and untaught). He then turned to His disciples and said privately to them "Blessed are those whose eyes see what you see! For I tell you that many prophets and kings longed to see what you see and they did not see it, and to hear what you hear and did not hear it" (Luke 10:23-24). Although Jesus in this instance is talking about the absolute greatness and demonstration of His power, the principle is same. God does what He says.

Looking back, I needn't have wasted my time worrying about the whats, ifs and maybes but enjoyed the ride. I have come to realise that the Bible gives you choices, "let not your heart be troubled," in other words, worrying is a choice. God is always true to His word. It's not for any small reason that He tells us with such confidence what our attitude should be like. After all, He is the maker of heaven and earth and continually watches over us for our benefit.

Today you have choices, just as I have. Choose to trust in the one who is called Faithful and True.

Call to Action Prayer

Do not let your hearts be troubled (depressed or agitated). You believe in and trust and trust in and rely on God; believe in and trust also on Me. In my Father's house there are many dwelling places (homes). If it were not so, I would have told you; for I am going away to prepare a place for you.

John 1:1-2 Amplified Bible

Father God, thank you for the truth of your Word that tells me that you have already gone ahead of me to prepare what I need in all areas of my life. Please forgive me for worrying and not believing you. Today I make a decision not to worry or fret about things but to trust you and Jesus. I pray that when I am tempted to worry that you will remind me that you've got everything covered, in Jesus name. Amen.

Notes

CONCLUSION
Arise, take my hand and come with me.

My Beloved speaks and says to me, rise up my love, my fair one and come away. For behold the winter is past; the rain is over and gone. The flowers appear on the earth; the time for singing has come, and the voice of the turtle dove is heard in the land.
Song of Solomon 2:10-12

As I come to this stage in the journey and reflect on the goodness of God I am struck once again by His loving kindness. The journey from brokenness to wholeness, sadness to joy and lostness to foundness was really about the lover of my soul wooing me into his presence.

If you are unsure if God is willing to heal you, you are not alone. In Luke 5:13, a man full of leprosy approached Jesus to find out if Jesus would be willing to heal him. He said, "If you are willing, You are able to cure me. And Jesus reached out His hand and touched him, saying I am willing; be cleansed! And immediately the leprosy left him."

It is interesting to note that the man didn't doubt whether Jesus had the ability to heal him, obviously that had been settled in his mind, the real question was whether Jesus would see him and his situation as important enough to merit attention. The Bible tells us in Mark 1:41 that Jesus' response was one of compassion and that Jesus not only touched and healed him but spoke specifically to his doubt to reassure him. When we go to Jesus He does more than heal us. He extends his hands towards us, speaks directly to what is bothering us. In Psalm 138, King David says "The Lord will perfect that which concerns me." In other words, I'm confident that my concerns are on God's agenda so they will be addressed.

I want to encourage you my friend to never doubt God's willingness to heal you. My question to you is are you willing to go to Him? Today he says to you I AM willing and He extends His hand of love to you.

HEALING MINISTERIES

Sozo Ministries International
Dunwood Oaks
Danes Road
Awbridge
Romsey
Hampshire
SO51 0GF
England

Telephone +44 (0)1794 344920
Email: email@sozo.org

Borderline Counselling Service
42a Warwick Road
Carlisle
CA1 1DN

Telephone: +44 (0)1288 596900
Email: info@borderlinecounselling.co.uk

Notes